D0479109

Messing
BAKING

A Childr
Activity

BAZI 090

...n.com

...book for your
...f your book's
...me yellowed
...east, in good

Messing Around with
BAKING CHEMISTRY
A Children's Museum
Activity Book

by Bernie Zubrowski

Illustrated by Signe Hanson

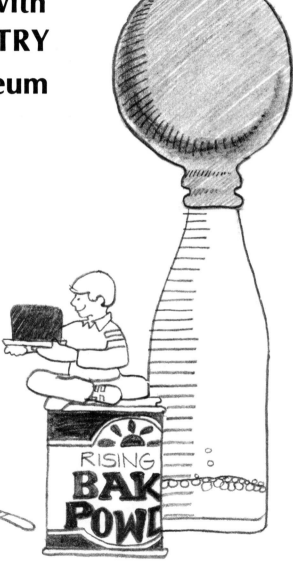

Little, Brown and Company
Boston   Toronto   London

Library of Congress Cataloging in Publication Data

Zubrowski, Bernie.
  Messing around with baking chemistry.

  (A Children's Museum activity book)
  SUMMARY: Presents experiments and projects to
explore what happens when batter and dough turn
into cake and bread. Emphasizes the properties
of baking powder, baking soda, and yeast.
  1. Cake – Juvenile literature. 2. Baking –
Juvenile literature. [1. Baking – Experiments.
2. Experiments. 3. Chemistry] I. Hanson, Signe.
II. Title. III. Series: Children's Museum
activity book.
TX771.Z76   641.8'653   81-4291
ISBN 0-316-98879-0 (pbk.)

*Published simultaneously in Canada
by Little, Brown & Company (Canada) Limited*

PRINTED IN THE UNITED STATES OF AMERICA

10 9 8 7 6

To my many young friends at the Philip School
in Watertown, Massachusetts, and my two daughters,
Nicole and Selena, who have made great messes
with me in experimenting with cake baking.

INTRODUCTION

Baking is lots of fun. You get to mix lots of things together, put the mixture into an oven, and, of course, you get to eat the result afterward. But this is only part of it. There are all sorts of experiments that one can do as part of this process. Have you ever baked a cake from scratch? That is, you measure out and mix together all the ingredients yourself instead of using a prepared mix from a store. There is a lot of science you can learn while cooking. All it takes is an adventurous mind and the practice of looking closely at what is happening.

What this book is about is how to investigate the chemistry of cake and bread making. There is a mystery involved. Somehow the batter or dough starts out small and expands. In fact, bread dough can expand to twice its original size!

So, read on and find out more about this mystery as well as others that will come up as you try out the different recipes and experiments.

EXPERIMENTING WITH CAKE RECIPES

If you look in a number of cookbooks, you will find many recipes for cakes. Although there are many sorts of cakes, all are made in basically the same way with similar kinds of ingredients. Check this out. Look at a bunch of recipes and see what the common ingredients are.

Here is a list that I came up with:

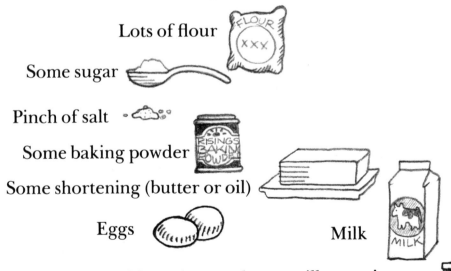

Lots of flour

Some sugar

Pinch of salt

Some baking powder

Some shortening (butter or oil)

Eggs

Milk

Some sort of flavoring, such as vanilla or spices

You can start off by following one of the recipes in a cookbook, or you can make up one of your own. If you haven't made a cake before, the following recipe is a simple one that you can start with. Then you can experiment with this recipe to see what other kinds of cakes you can make.

Since you are experimenting, it is a good idea to work with small quantities or proportions and make small cakes. Cupcake size is a little too small. Something the size of a soup bowl is just about right. Have an adult help you when turning on the heat in the oven.

MATERIALS NEEDED:

Aluminum foil	Milk
Flour	Cooking oil
Sugar	Vanilla
Salt	Egg
Baking powder	Measuring spoons

Set the oven at 350°. (Most cakes are baked around 325°–375°.) Have an adult turn it on.

You can make a small pan for baking the cake in the following manner:

Find a bowl that is wider than it is high.

Then take aluminum foil and wrap it around the bowl to form a pan.

You will have to use several sheets to make it strong enough to hold the batter. Oil the sheets with cooking oil or shortening before making the pan, so the cake will come out easily after baking. Place this inside a metal pan, such as a pie pan, to provide more support, and in case there are any spills.

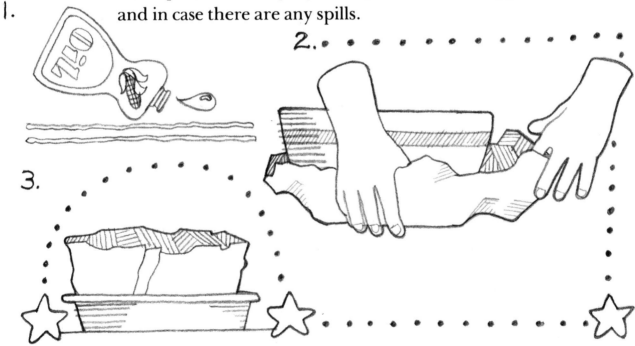

1.

2.

3.

Since you are going to make a small cake, you should measure out the ingredients in tablespoons rather than cups. This means that instead of measuring 2 or 3 cups of flour, you might measure out 6 tablespoons of it. The quantity of sugar should be a little less than half the flour, so measure out 3 tablespoons of sugar. Salt and baking powder are only a very small proportion of the total ingredients. Add just a pinch of salt and two or three pinches of baking powder.

The liquid part of the batter is smaller than the dry part. About 2 tablespoons each of milk and cooking oil could be used. For a cake of this size, a whole egg would be too much. Break an egg into a cup, beat it until it is mixed, and use only part of it. You'll need only a few drops of flavoring such as vanilla.

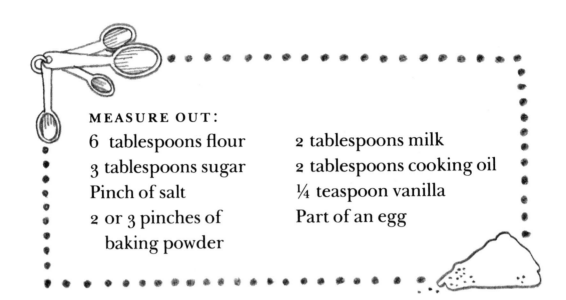

MEASURE OUT:

6 tablespoons flour	2 tablespoons milk
3 tablespoons sugar	2 tablespoons cooking oil
Pinch of salt	¼ teaspoon vanilla
2 or 3 pinches of baking powder	Part of an egg

Mix the dry with the wet ingredients well.

Once you have measured out and mixed the ingredients, pour the batter into the pan you made and place that pan very carefully in the oven, remembering that the racks are *very* hot.

Bake about fifteen minutes. Keep a watch so that the cake doesn't burn, but don't open the oven door often. Test the middle of the cake by pushing a toothpick into it. If the toothpick comes out clean, the cake is done.

Now, here is where you can begin to experiment. Make another cake, but leave out some of the ingredients and see what happens. For instance, what would happen if you left out the eggs, or if you left out the baking powder? In doing this kind of experiment you can track down which ingredient or ingredients help make the batter expand.

Here are suggested recipes for experimenting.
Follow the same procedure as before.

1. 6 tbsp. flour
   3 tbsp. sugar
   Pinch of salt
   2 or 3 pinches
      baking powder
   2 tbsp. milk
   Part of an egg
   ¼ tsp. vanilla
   (Leave out oil.)

2. 6 tbsp. flour
   3 tbsp. sugar
   Pinch of salt
   2 or 3 pinches
      baking powder
   2 tbsp. milk
   2 tbsp. cooking oil
   ¼ tsp. vanilla
   (Leave out egg.)

3. 6 tbsp. flour
   3 tbsp. sugar
   Pinch of salt
   2 tbsp. milk
   2 tbsp. cooking oil
   Part of an egg
   ¼ tsp. vanilla
   (Leave out baking
      powder.)

THE SPECIAL POWER OF BAKING POWDER

If you have experimented with trying different cake recipes and eliminating the different ingredients, you probably found out that the batter doesn't rise very much when baking powder isn't present.

Baking powder is a key ingredient in cakes, because it makes the batter expand. If you play with baking powder by itself you will find that it does some very curious things.

Let's find out more about baking powder.

What happens when baking powder is added to different liquids?

Try mixing it with the following liquids and record what happens.

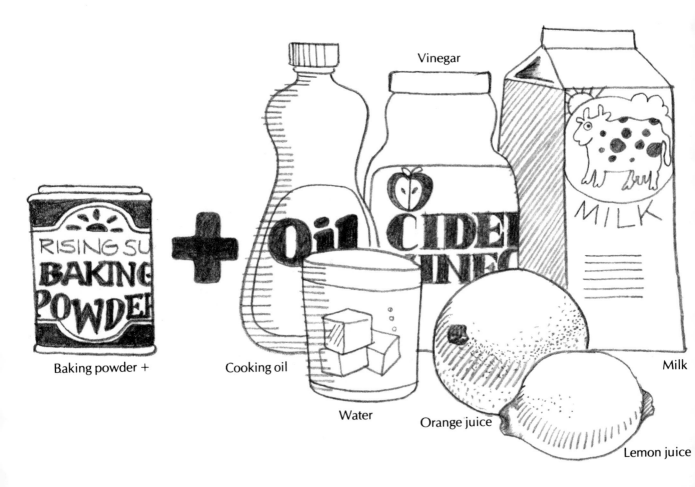

Baking powder +

Cooking oil

Water

Vinegar

Orange juice

Lemon juice

Milk

Try mixing it with cold and then hot water. Is there any difference?

Can you think of other liquids you could use to get the baking powder to fizz? Are there other powders around the kitchen that might do the same thing?

After you have dropped baking powder into a jar or bottle with a liquid, quickly place your hand on the opening and keep it there. What happens after a few minutes?

Now here is something special to try that will show you what happens to the baking powder when it is added to the cake batter.

Fill up two glasses with hot water. In one, put some dishwashing detergent (1 tsp.) and stir. Add a tablespoon of baking powder to each and stir with separate spoons.

Now watch carefully.

With a magnifying glass look at the sides of the glass.

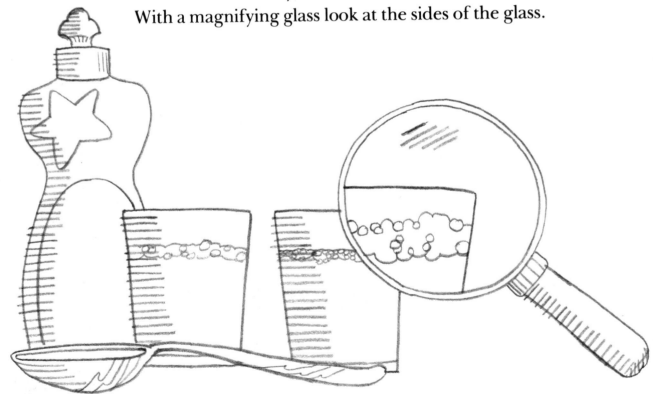

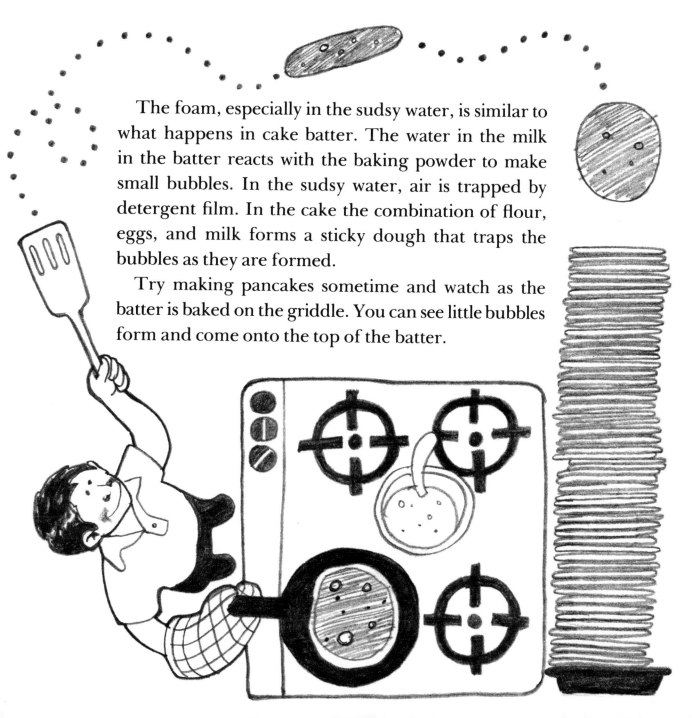

The foam, especially in the sudsy water, is similar to what happens in cake batter. The water in the milk in the batter reacts with the baking powder to make small bubbles. In the sudsy water, air is trapped by detergent film. In the cake the combination of flour, eggs, and milk forms a sticky dough that traps the bubbles as they are formed.

Try making pancakes sometime and watch as the batter is baked on the griddle. You can see little bubbles form and come onto the top of the batter.

Capturing the Gas from Baking Powder

There is another way of capturing the air that is released when baking powder reacts with liquids.

In the last experiment, we saw that mixing baking powder with detergent water produced lots of gas bubbles that were trapped by the detergent film. But what happens to the gas produced by the baking powder and regular water? This experiment shows how you can trap the gas that is released when baking powder reacts with other liquids.

MATERIALS NEEDED:
    Narrow-neck bottles, such as soda bottles
    Balloons (big, round-shaped ones work the best)
    Baking powder
    Funnel
    Hot and cold water

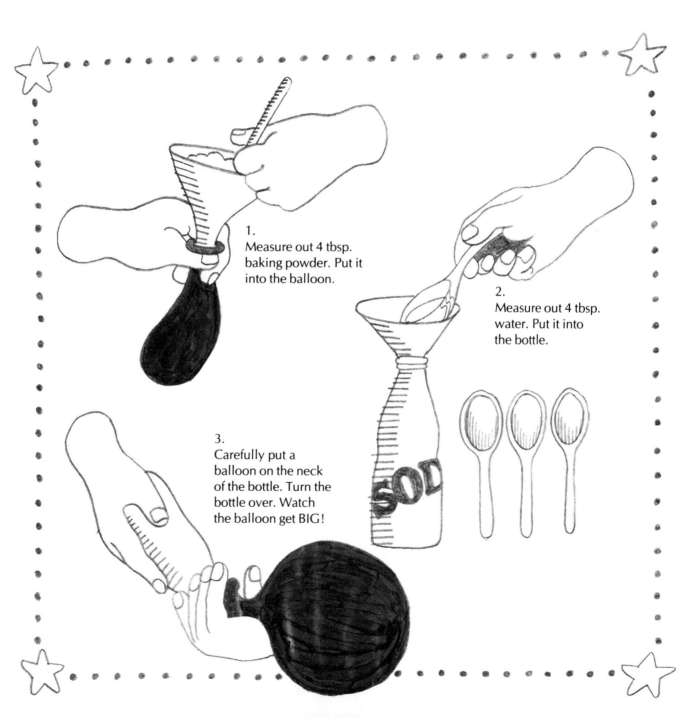

1.
Measure out 4 tbsp. baking powder. Put it into the balloon.

2.
Measure out 4 tbsp. water. Put it into the bottle.

3.
Carefully put a balloon on the neck of the bottle. Turn the bottle over. Watch the balloon get BIG!

SOD

If you have a bunch of bottles all alike, there are several experiments you can try.

For instance:

Does the amount of water in the bottle make a difference in the final size of the balloon?

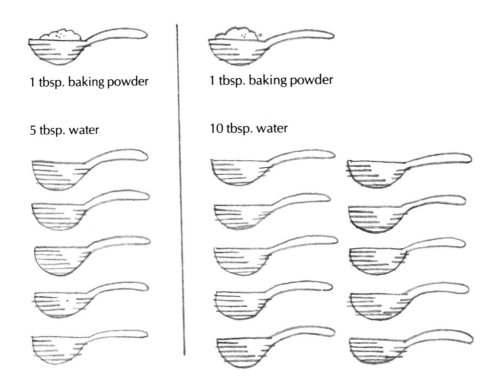

1 tbsp. baking powder   1 tbsp. baking powder

5 tbsp. water   10 tbsp. water

Does the amount of baking powder in the balloon make a difference in how big it gets?

Will other liquids blow up the balloon? Try vinegar, cooking oil, orange juice, lemon juice.

Do some brands of baking powder blow up the balloon more and some less?

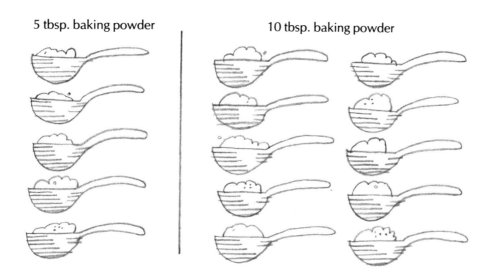

5 tbsp. baking powder   10 tbsp. baking powder

Heating Up Air

The balloon on top of the bottle and the film from soapy or detergent water act in the same way as the flour and egg in the cake baking. In each situation the gas is trapped as it is made.

When you put a cake in the oven the mixture expands. What will happen if you put an empty soda bottle with a balloon on top in some hot water?

1. Place an empty balloon on top of the bottle.
2. Put the bottle into a saucepan of cool water.
3. Heat the saucepan slowly with a low flame.

What happens to the balloon as the water heats up?
Caution: Let the bottle cool in the pot before taking it out.

BAKING SODA IN CAKES

You might have noticed that on your kitchen shelf there is not only baking powder, but also baking soda. Are these the same thing? Do they give the same results when baking? Is there just a difference in name or are they really different?

If you go back to your cookbook and look again at the different cake recipes, you will find that in fact some recipes call for baking soda instead of baking powder. Try making one of these cakes and see what happens. Here is a recipe for chocolate cake that uses baking soda. When mixing the ingredients and baking the cake, watch carefully and see if there is any difference compared to the other cakes that you have made.

MIX TOGETHER:
1 ⅔ cup flour
1 cup sugar
½ cup cocoa
1 teaspoon salt
1 ½ teaspoons baking soda

BEAT IN WITH A SPOON:
1 cup buttermilk or
   sour milk
½ cup shortening
1 ½ teaspoons vanilla

Stir all this until mixed well.
Pour it into the oiled pan.
Bake for about 30 minutes, until done. The cake is done when the surface comes back up if you press it with one finger.

Taking a Close Look at Baking Soda

In the recipe with baking soda there was one ingredient that was different from previous recipes, and it was an important one. Sour milk or buttermilk was used instead of regular milk. There is a special reason for this. Try the following experiments and watch carefully what happens when you mix the liquids and powders together.

We've seen that mixing baking powder with different liquids caused some of the liquids to fizz. Now try the same thing with baking soda.

In glasses or jars, mix baking soda with water, milk, cooking oil, vinegar, sour milk, orange juice, lemon juice.

Which combination fizzes? Which doesn't?

How does this behavior compare with that of baking soda?

Do both fizz with the same liquids?

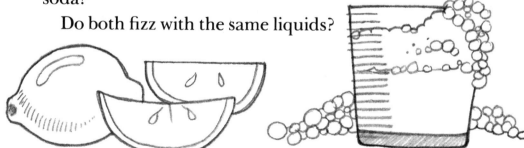

If you look at the list of ingredients on the packages of baking soda and baking powder, you will find something interesting. Baking soda has another name: sodium bicarbonate. If you look at the labels of different kinds of baking powder you will find that there is one ingredient that is the same in all of them: it's sodium bicarbonate.

In fact, what is curious is that Alka-Seltzer, Bromo-Seltzer and denture cleanser, and many other powders that fizz when added to water, all have sodium bicarbonate in them. So there is something special about sodium bicarbonate.

Remember that the recipe for the baking soda cake called for sour milk. Also, when you mixed baking soda with some liquids, the ones like vinegar and lemon juice fizzed a lot. What these liquids have in common is that they are all acids.

28

Now, here is a test to see if baking soda reacts the same way with other kinds of acids. Cream of tartar is another name for tartaric acid; sour salt is also called citric acid. (These are available at most supermarkets.) Put some cream of tartar in water, stir, then add the baking soda. Follow the same procedure with sour salt in another glass.

Does each of these combinations fizz?

This is a useful thing to know. We can say now that sodium bicarbonate fizzes not just with vinegar and lemon juice, but that it fizzes with acids also.

So, if you want to bake a cake with baking soda, you need to add some ingredient that is acid. For instance, if you want to make an orange cake, you can add orange peel and orange juice for flavoring, but the juice will also help make the cake rise.

A CONTEST:

Now, let's compare baking soda and baking powder to each other. When you mix baking soda with vinegar, it really fizzes a lot, which means that a lot of gas is being made. Baking powder also fizzes a lot when you add vinegar to it. Which of these powders would you guess gives off most gas?

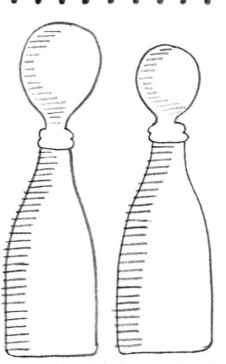

One way of measuring this is to go back and do the experiment with the balloons again (see page 21). Put equal amounts of baking powder and soda in each balloon and equal amounts of vinegar in the bottles. Use the same kind of balloons on both bottles and tip them over at the same time. Then watch to see if you can tell if one has gotten bigger than the other after a few minutes.

Here's a more accurate way of measuring the amount of gas.

Comparing inflated balloons is not an accurate way of comparing amounts of gases. Sometimes balloons will have the same amount of gas in them, although they have different shapes. The drawing shows another way of measuring the gas coming from baking soda or baking powder.

MATERIALS NEEDED:

Plastic tubing: 2 meters (6 feet, from hardware store or aquarium supply store)

Sponge rubber ball

Jar with opening in which ball fits snugly

2 barrels from ball-point pens

Gallon jar

Large bucket

or dishpan

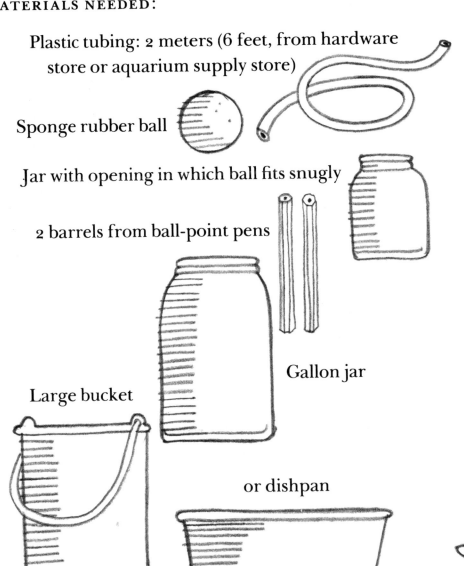

A. Assembling a Gas Generator

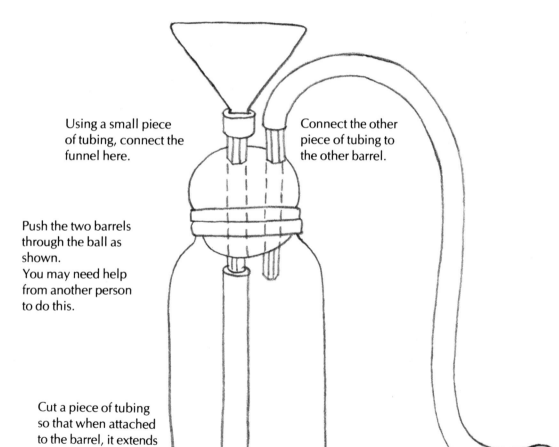

Using a small piece of tubing, connect the funnel here.

Connect the other piece of tubing to the other barrel.

Push the two barrels through the ball as shown.
You may need help from another person to do this.

Cut a piece of tubing so that when attached to the barrel, it extends to the very bottom of the bottle.

B. Setting Up a Collection System

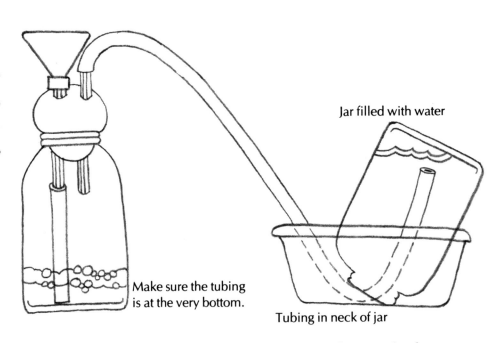

Jar filled with water

Make sure the tubing is at the very bottom.

Tubing in neck of jar

1. Measure out 2 tbsp. baking powder and place in jar.
2. Put stopper (ball) on tightly.
3. Measure out 2 tbsp. water or vinegar into glass.
4. Pour liquid into funnel.

If there are no leaks in your system, the gas will push water out of the jar.

Measure with a ruler how much gas came into the gallon jug and record the result.

With this kind of arrangement there are all kinds of experiments you can do.

First of all, see whether equal quantities of baking soda and baking powder produce equal quantities of gas with water and with vinegar.

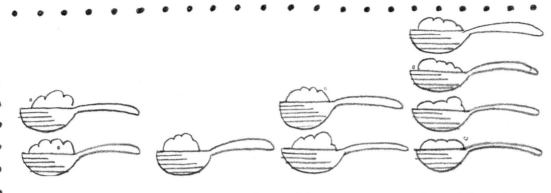

Here are some other things you can do with this special arrangement.

If you start off with two tablespoons of baking soda in the small bottle, can you keep adding vinegar to this powder and still make gas? Will the gas eventually fill the whole gallon jug?

Starting over,

With 1 teaspoon of baking soda and ⅓ cup of water, how much gas?

With 2 teaspoons of baking soda and ⅓ cup of water will you get twice as much gas?

With 4 teaspoons will you get four times as much?

If you use equal quantities of different kinds of baking powder do you always get the same amount of gas when water is added?

What happens if you use cold water, warm water, or very hot water to add to the baking powder?

Will you still get as much gas after heating baking powder and mixing it with water? Will you get any?

Remember when comparing different powders or the different liquids always to use the same amount of powders and the same amounts of liquids.

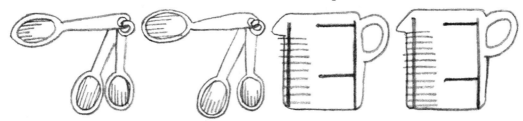

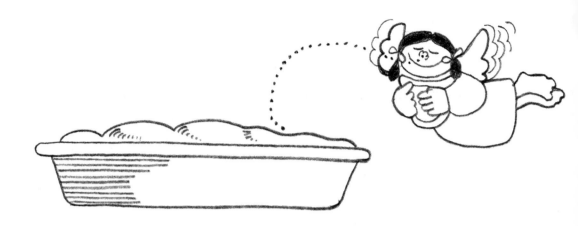

Baking Soda Bread

Baking soda is not only used for making cakes; it can also be used in bread. The recipes are similar to the ones for cakes but have fewer ingredients. One of the simplest types of bread to make with baking soda is Irish soda bread.

MATERIALS NEEDED:

4 cups flour   1 teaspoon salt
1 teaspoon baking soda   1 ½ cups buttermilk
optional: 1 cup raisins

Set oven at 375°.

1. Mix all dry ingredients together.

2. Pour buttermilk into the center of the ingredients. First, mix thoroughly with a big spoon. Add raisins if you like. Then work the dough with your hands for a few minutes.

3. Put this dough into a metal pan (such as a pie pan) that has been lightly oiled, forming the dough into a circular mass about an inch thick.

4. Bake for 35 or 40 minutes, testing the center of the dough with a toothpick at the end of the time to see if it is done.

Like all bread, it is tastiest right after it comes out of the oven. Get butter and jam ready so you can enjoy this special flavor and smell.

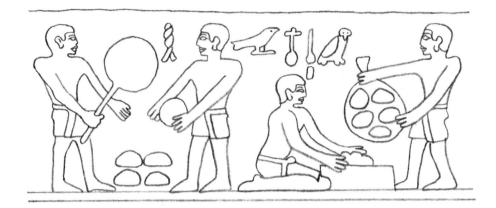

Getting Dough to Rise Another Way

Flour mixed with a few other ingredients and baking powder will give you expanded dough when placed in an oven, but there are other ways of getting the same result. In fact, up until a little more than a hundred years ago, sodium bicarbonate was not used in baking at all. It was put into use only in the early 1800s.

However, people have been making bread for thousands of years. Dried-out loaves that were made about six thousand years ago were found in Egyptian pyramids. People of ancient times discovered that when a mixture of flour and water is left standing around, it rises on its own. They found that something carried by the air caused it to happen. Eventually, people like Louis Pasteur and other scientists found that the cause of this was a very small living organism which is called yeast.

If you haven't made yeast bread before, you should try it. It is lots of fun to knead the bread and it isn't difficult to do. What is so mysterious is how the dough gets bigger and bigger as the yeast grows. Here is one way of making bread.

MATERIALS NEEDED:

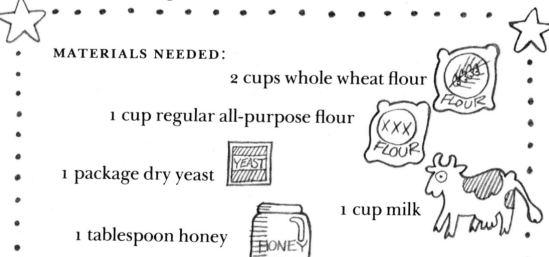

2 cups whole wheat flour

1 cup regular all-purpose flour

1 package dry yeast

1 cup milk

1 tablespoon honey

1 tablespoon butter or margarine

1 teaspoon salt

1. In a large bowl combine the yeast with ½ cup of whole wheat flour and ½ cup of the other flour.

2. Use a saucepan that will hold all of the milk, honey, margarine, and salt. Heat this mixture slowly till the margarine melts. Make sure it is *not* hot but only warm. Then add it to the flour and yeast mixture.

3. Using a big spoon, stir till the wet and dry ingredients are mixed thoroughly. Then gradually stir in the rest of the two kinds of flour till the dough is stiff. You may have some flour left over. Save this for when you are kneading.

4. The next step is to knead the dough on a clean table or board with flour sprinkled on it. (Kneading is hard to describe, so you should ask your mom or dad about this part.) The idea is to keep folding the dough over and over on itself. This is usually done for about 10 minutes.

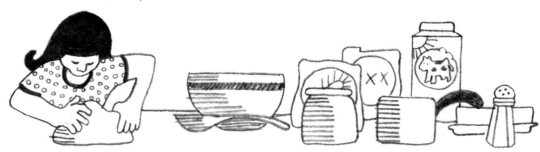

5. Now, here is the curious part. Shape the dough into a ball and put it into a big bowl that has been oiled. Cover it with a cloth and let the bowl stand in a warm place for about an hour and a half. The lump of dough should be about twice its original size then!

6. Take this dough and punch it down on the floured surface. This time, put it into an oiled bread pan, and again let it sit in a warm place, covered with a dry cloth, for about an hour.

7. Now that the dough has expanded twice, it is ready for baking. Bake at 375° for 45 to 50 minutes.

With some of the dough that you have made, you can try the following experiment. Break off three small portions of the dough, making sure they are all the same size. Put them into three glasses or jars, all the same size. Put a rubber band around the glass where the top of the dough is.

Place one in the refrigerator and one on top of a stove or radiator where it is very warm (or in a pot of very warm water). Leave the third one on the kitchen table.

Check occasionally, and see how much the dough has risen. How much difference does hot or warm temperature make?

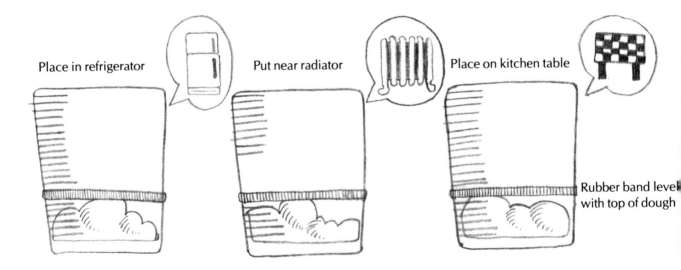

Place in refrigerator

Put near radiator

Place on kitchen table

Rubber band level with top of dough

Capturing Yeast Gas

On the previous pages, we saw how baking soda can be mixed with vinegar inside a soda bottle to inflate a balloon. Since yeast can make dough rise in making bread, it also might make balloons inflate.

Here are some experiments to try to see if this can happen.

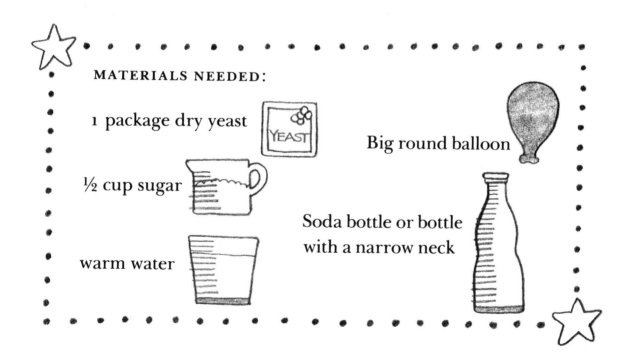

MATERIALS NEEDED:

1 package dry yeast

½ cup sugar

warm water

Big round balloon

Soda bottle or bottle with a narrow neck

1. Mix the sugar and yeast well with warm water in the bottle, making sure the sugar has dissolved.

2. Put the balloon on top of the bottle and wait fifteen minutes to a half hour for results. You should start to see bubbles rising in the liquid, and soon the balloon will start to inflate.

How long does the solution bubble? Will there be enough gas to break the balloon?

SAME MATERIALS AS ABOVE.

1. Place sugar and yeast in each bottle, mixing them well. Then add cold water to one, warm to another, and very hot water to the third bottle. Be very careful with the hot water. Use a holder to hold the bottle.

2. Wait one minute and then put a balloon on each and wait an hour.

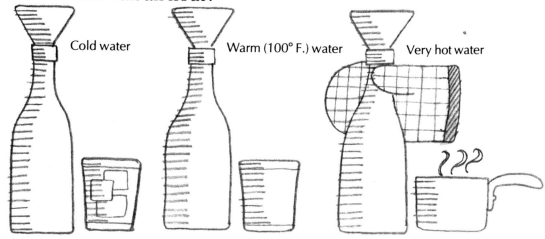

Cold water   Warm (100° F.) water   Very hot water

In each book that tells how to make bread they say that it is important to have warm water for the yeast. Here is something to try to see why this is so.

If you have followed all the steps carefully, you will find that up to a point, the warmer the temperature the faster the gas is generated, but if the water is too hot, as in the situation where very hot water is added, no gas is produced.

Yeast are living organisms. As with other living things, they are killed once the temperature gets too high. This is why no gas is produced when very hot water is used.

Other Foods for Yeast

As you saw in the previous experiment, the yeast acted on the sugar, using it as a food. In doing so, it made alcohol as well as a gas. This particular situation has been taken advantage of to make all sorts of wines and beers. People thousands of years ago discovered that if crushed fruits, vegetables, and wheat and other grains were allowed to sit in water, the mixture would bubble and eventually make a beer or wine. Since then it has been discovered that the fermentation was caused by yeast. Using some materials around the kitchen, you can do further experiments with yeast.

Honey

Grape juice

Flour

Molasses

Soda bottles

Balloons

Yeast

½ cup honey

1 pkg. yeast

warm water
to top

½ cup
molasses

1 pkg. yeast

warm water

½ cup flour

1 pkg. yeast

warm water

1 cup grape
juice

1 pkg. yeast

warm water

It will take a while for some of these to start bubbling (about half an hour). Once they all start bubbling, see if they all make gas at the same rate. Also, see how long each continues to bubble.

Measuring the Amount of Yeast Gas

Depending upon the amount of sugar you add to the water, and the temperature of the room, different amounts of gas will be given off. In fact, this action can sometimes continue over several days. It depends on how much of each material you started with, especially the amount of sugar.

To get some idea how much gas is produced, you can use an arrangement similar to the one on page 36. There will have to be some changes, but they are not major. Instead of two tubings, you only need one, and this is connected to the bottle by a piece of balloon.

The next technique is not as accurate because the gas dissolves in water. However, it is still useful because you may be surprised how much gas actually is made.

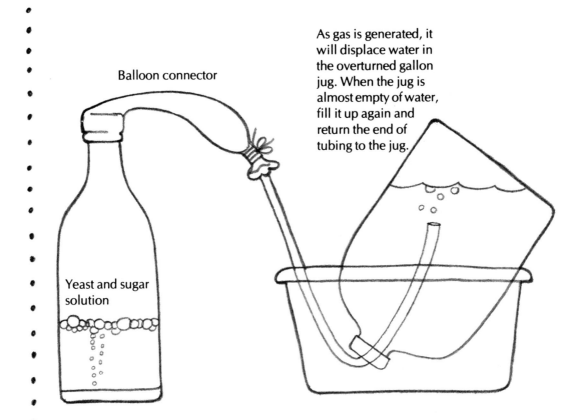

Balloon connector

As gas is generated, it will displace water in the overturned gallon jug. When the jug is almost empty of water, fill it up again and return the end of tubing to the jug.

Yeast and sugar solution

Keep this going for several days and see how much gas is made.

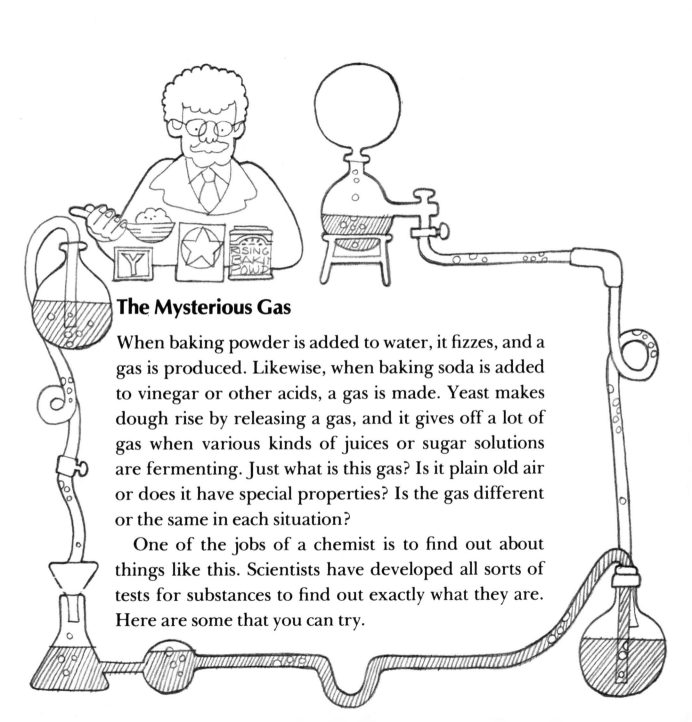

The Mysterious Gas

When baking powder is added to water, it fizzes, and a gas is produced. Likewise, when baking soda is added to vinegar or other acids, a gas is made. Yeast makes dough rise by releasing a gas, and it gives off a lot of gas when various kinds of juices or sugar solutions are fermenting. Just what is this gas? Is it plain old air or does it have special properties? Is the gas different or the same in each situation?

One of the jobs of a chemist is to find out about things like this. Scientists have developed all sorts of tests for substances to find out exactly what they are. Here are some that you can try.

A. Does the Gas Burn?

1. Place a candle in a jar so that it can't tip over. Plasticene or modeling clay in the bottom of the jar will help.
2. Put several tablespoons of baking powder into the jar.
3. Light the candle.
4. Quickly add some water without getting it on the flame. Watch what happens to the flame.
5. Carry out the same procedure with:
    Baking soda and vinegar
    Baking soda and orange juice
    Baking soda and cream of tartar and water

6. Carefully place a burning candle into a wide-mouth jar in which yeast has been reacting with sugar and water.

What happens in all these situations? If you have been careful, you will find that the candle goes out. The gas won't let the flame burn. So, you see that the gas is different from room air.

B. Is the Gas Heavier or Lighter than Air?

Make several jars of the gas as shown on page 54.

Tilt the glass or jar as if pouring a liquid over the flame. You'll find that the flame will go out.

Does this happen with other combinations such as baking soda and orange juice?

C. Is the Gas Produced by Baking Powder and Water Acidic?

You can find out by bubbling the gas through a solution of bromo thymol blue (BTB). BTB is used to test solutions for acidity. You can buy it at an aquarium supply store.

Bubble the gas from baking powder and water through water that has a few drops of BTB in it.

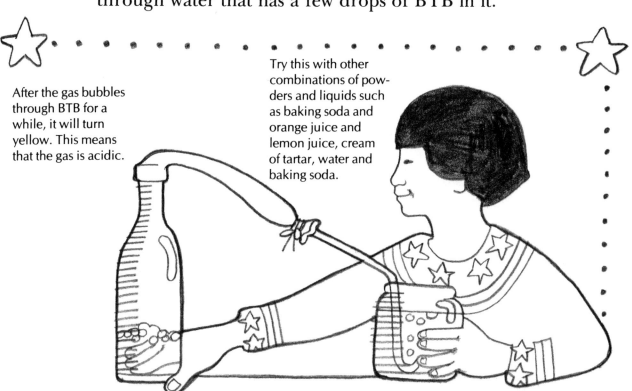

After the gas bubbles through BTB for a while, it will turn yellow. This means that the gas is acidic.

Try this with other combinations of powders and liquids such as baking soda and orange juice and lemon juice, cream of tartar, water and baking soda.

If you have done all these tests carefully, you will find that the gases from the different combinations give the same result. Each puts the fire out; each can be poured on burning candles to put them out; and each changes BTB from blue to yellow.

You might conclude from these experiments that the same gas is being made. In fact, each of the different combinations is producing a gas called carbon dioxide. You would need to do other tests to establish this fully, but the preceding ones are usually good indicators for carbon dioxide.

There is an important fact to remember about this. Yeast is a living organism, which happens to give off carbon dioxide in certain situations. Sodium bicarbonate is a chemical, and the way the gas is generated is very different from the way it is made by yeast.

(WITHOUT YEAST)

Scientists such as chemists have taken advantage of these similar results where a chemical can imitate nature. Nowadays, some breads are made without yeast. Instead, carbon dioxide is bubbled into water under pressure. This solution is similar to soda water. It is then mixed with dough under pressure in a special chamber, and allowed to expand. In this way the dough rises much more quickly than with yeast.

Of course, something is lost. The bread doesn't smell as good as yeast bread, and some people say it is less nutritious. So, we may gain some speed in making bread, but at the same time we lose out on something in choosing this method.

Carbonization

There is another interesting property of carbon dioxide that hasn't been mentioned so far. When you fermented grape juice and a sugar solution with yeast, it may have reminded you of soda water. When you pop the top off of a soda bottle, the soda is fizzy. Now that you know some tests for carbon dioxide, you can test this gas and see if that's what it is.

How Much Gas Is There in a Bottle of Soda?

Open a warm bottle of soda. If you put your finger on the top and shake it, the pressure is so great that gas and liquid come out. You may be surprised at how much gas is actually in a bottle of soda. Using the balloon technique on page 54 you can find out. Or do this in the following manner.

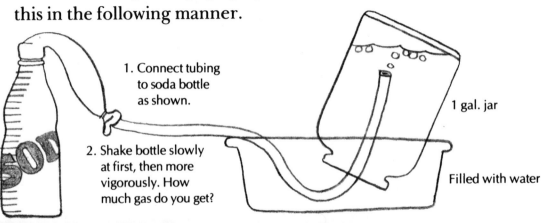

1. Connect tubing to soda bottle as shown.

2. Shake bottle slowly at first, then more vigorously. How much gas do you get?

1 gal. jar

Filled with water

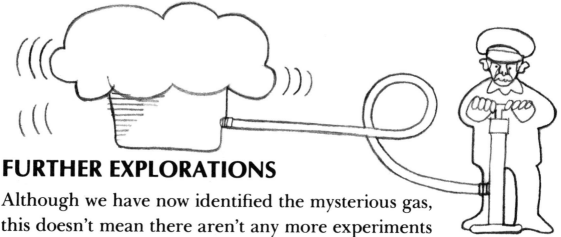

FURTHER EXPLORATIONS

Although we have now identified the mysterious gas, this doesn't mean there aren't any more experiments left to do. Alka-Seltzer fizzes in water. Does it fizz in other liquids? What are the ingredients of Alka-Seltzer? Are they similar to baking powder? What gas do you think is being generated when it fizzes?

Popovers are fun to make and eat. The recipe, giving ingredients and instructions on how to cook them, can be found in many cookbooks. There is no baking soda, baking powder, or yeast used, but somehow the batter puffs up and a hollow shell is formed. See if you can figure out how this happens. And always remember to take care, especially when handling hot objects. Just to be sure, have an adult around when you try these "experiments."

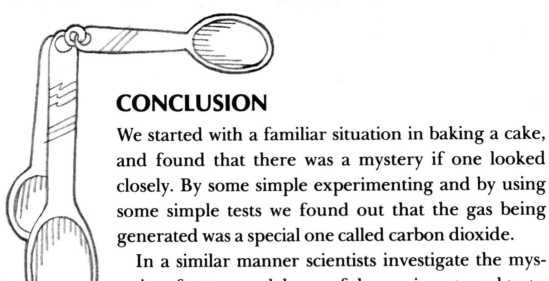

CONCLUSION

We started with a familiar situation in baking a cake, and found that there was a mystery if one looked closely. By some simple experimenting and by using some simple tests we found out that the gas being generated was a special one called carbon dioxide.

In a similar manner scientists investigate the mysteries of nature and, by careful experiments and tests, solve these mysteries. Cooking offers all kinds of opportunities for learning some basic physics and chemistry, so try your hand at it often, and along the way see what mysteries you can discover and then solve.

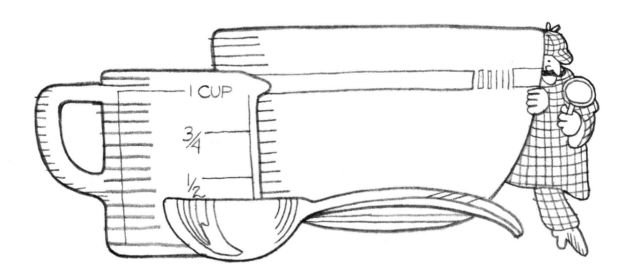